Grassland Animals

Badgers

by Patricia J. Murphy

Consulting Editor: Gail Saunders-Smith, Ph.D.
Consultant: Marsha A. Sovada, Ph.D., Research Wildlife Biologist
Northern Prairie Wildlife Research Center, U.S. Geological Survey
Jamestown, North Dakota

Capstone
press
Mankato, Minnesota

Pebble Books are published by Capstone Press
151 Good Counsel Drive, P.O. Box 669, Mankato, Minnesota 56002
www.capstonepress.com

1 2 3 4 5 6 09 08 07 06 05 04

Library of Congress Cataloging-in-Publication Data
Murphy, Patricia J., 1963–
    Badgers / by Patricia J. Murphy.
    p. cm.—(Grassland animals)
    Summary: Simple text and photographs introduce badgers and their grasslands
habitat.
    Includes bibliographical references and index.
    ISBN 0-7368-2071-X (hardcover)
    1. Badgers—Juvenile literature. [1. Badgers. 2. Grasslands.] I. Title. II. Series.
QL737.C25M85 2004
599.76′7—dc22   2003013411

Note to Parents and Teachers

The Grassland Animals series supports national science standards
related to life science. This book describes and illustrates badgers.
The photographs support early readers in understanding the text.
The repetition of words and phrases helps early readers learn new
words. This book also introduces early readers to subject-specific
vocabulary words, which are defined in the Glossary. Early readers
may need assistance to read some words and to use the Table of
Contents, Glossary, Read More, Internet Sites, and Index/Word List
sections of the book.

Table of Contents

Badgers

Badgers are mammals.
Badgers have sharp teeth
and long snouts.

Badgers have white and black face patches called badges.

Badgers have thick fur.
Their fur is black, gray,
brown, and white.

Badgers puff up their fur when danger is near. Badgers also give off a musky smell.

Badgers have strong legs and long claws. Badgers dig with their claws.

areas where badgers live

Where Badgers Live

Badgers live on grasslands. Grasslands are large open areas of grass.

What Badgers Do

Badgers dig burrows to live in. Most badgers live alone.

Badgers eat small mammals, earthworms, insects, and plants. Badgers dig to find food at night.

Badgers rest in burrows during the day. Burrows are cool in summer and warm in winter.

Glossary

badge—a marking on the face of a badger; badgers are named for these markings.

burrow—a tunnel or hole in the ground made by badgers or other small mammals

claw—a hard, curved nail on a foot of an animal; badgers use their claws to dig.

fur—the soft, thick hairy coat of an animal

musky—a strong, sharp smell; scent glands near a badger's tail give off a musky smell.

mammal—a warm-blooded animal that has a backbone; mammals have fur or hair; female mammals feed milk to their young.

patch—a small part or area

snout—the long front part of an animal's face; the snout includes the nose, mouth, and jaws.

Read More

Johnson, Rebecca L. *A Walk in the Prairie.* Biomes of North America. Minneapolis: Carolrhoda, 2001.

Robinson, W. Wright. *How Mammals Build Their Amazing Homes.* Animal Architects. Woodbridge, Conn.: Blackbirch Press, 1999.

Internet Sites

FactHound offers a safe, fun way to find Internet sites related to this book. All of the sites on FactHound have been researched by our staff.

Here's how:

1. Visit *www.facthound.com*
2. Type in this special code **073682071X** for age-appropriate sites. Or enter a search word related to this book for a more general search.
3. Click on the **Fetch It** button.

FactHound will fetch the best sites for you!

Index/Word List

Word Count: 111
Early-Intervention Level: 13

Editorial Credits

Martha E. H. Rustad, editor; Patrick Dentinger, designer; Scott Thoms, photo researcher; Karen Risch, product planning editor

Photo Credits

Bruce Coleman Inc./Joe McDonald, 4
Comstock Klips, 16
Corel, 12
Erwin and Peggy Bauer, 20
EyeWire Images, cover
Kent and Donna Dannen, 10
Malie Rich-Griffith/infocusphotos.com, 1
McDonald Wildlife Photography/Joe McDonald, 6
Peggy Patterson/GeoIMAGERY, 8
Tom and Pat Leeson, 18
Tom Stack & Associates/Joe McDonald, 14